Lernkrimi Hörbuch Englisch

The Butterworth Mystery

Alison Romer

compact

Diese Geschichte ist bereits als Lernkrimi Kurzkrimi „Stolen Summer" im Band „Blood & Breakfast", ISBN 978-3-8174-7760-9, erschienen.

Redaktion: Helga Aichele
Fachkorrektur: Fiona Cain
Produktion: Johannes Buchmann
Titelillustration: Karl Knospe
Typografischer Entwurf: EKH Werbeagentur GbR, textum GmbH
Umschlaggestaltung: EKH Werbeagentur GbR

ISBN 978-3-8174-8203-0
381748203/1

www.compactverlag.de, www.lernkrimi.de

Vorwort

Liebe Leserin, lieber Leser,

sicher zum Lernerfolg – mit Spaß und Spannung! Die Compact Lernkrimi Hörbücher mit ihrer Kombination aus vertonter Lektüre und didaktischem Übungsanteil eignen sich hervorragend, um breite Sprachkompetenzen in der Fremdsprache zu erwerben. Durch die authentische, zugleich aber dem Lernniveau angepasste Vertonung wird das Hörverstehen geschult. Die spannende Handlung, das angemessene Sprachniveau und die hörtextbezogenen Übungen fördern und motivieren den Lerner. Entwickelt nach neuesten Erkenntnissen der Fremdsprachendidaktik, sind Compact Lernkrimi Hörbücher das ideale Medium für einen Lernerfolg im Selbststudium.

So lernen Sie mit Compact Lernkrimi Hörbüchern:

- **Mit Begeisterung lernen:** Die packende Krimihandlung motiviert Sie – ob beim Hören, Lesen oder Mitlesen der englischen Originallektüre.
- **Wissen intensivieren und erweitern:** Mit der CD können Sie Ihr Hörverstehen gezielt verbessern. Mit den didaktisierten Hörtexten und den textbezogenen Übungen testen und trainieren Sie Ihre Sprachkenntnisse effektiv.
- **Systematisch lernen mit der Reihe Compact Lernkrimis:** Knüpfen Sie an Ihr individuelles Sprachniveau an und setzen Sie eigene Lernziele – linear im Schwierigkeitsgrad ansteigend oder mit punktuellen Schwerpunkten wie Grundwortschatz oder Hörverstehen.
- **Unabhängig sein:** Lernen Sie ganz individuell – wo und wann Sie wollen.

Viel Spaß beim **spannend Englisch lernen**
wünscht Ihnen

Prof. Dr. Christiane Neveling
Didaktik der romanischen Sprachen, Universität Leipzig

Inhalt

Zu diesem Buch

In einem Dorf in Lancashire werden Gemälde eines berühmten Künstlers aus einer Galerie gestohlen. Dabei verletzen die Diebe eine Museumswärterin schwer und entkommen unerkannt.

Sergeant Rose tappt zunächst im Dunkeln, aber dann weisen die Bilder selbst auf das Motiv hin. Kann er das Rätsel rechtzeitig lüften, um die Gemälde sicherzustellen?

1 Scary Stories

Michael Rose had been working for the Lancashire Police for seven years. He loved his job. Because he lived and worked in a small village, he knew many people by name. Even though he was only thirty-three, he was an **old-fashioned** type of policeman: friendly, caring and ready to help. He liked the people of Pendle Lee, and the people of Pendle Lee liked Sergeant Rose.

Crime was not a big problem. At the police station, days went by quite slowly. Many other officers liked to be in a bigger town or a city. But Michael loved being part of a small **community**. The village itself was also a lovely place to live. The church, which was in the centre, had been built in 1376. Many of the houses had been standing for a very long time. Even the pub, which was called "The White **Witch**", was hundreds of years old. At the **edge** of the village a river **flowed** through the fields and woods. On summer evenings it was as beautiful as a painting.

old-fashioned	altmodisch
crime	Verbrechen
community	Gemeinschaft
witch	Hexe
edge	Rand, Ecke
to flow	fließen
to deal with	sich beschäftigen mit, zu tun haben mit

However, there was not very much for young people to do. Bored teenagers were often getting into trouble. In fact, most of the problems Michael had to **deal with** were caused by teenagers. Loud music, graffiti and bad behaviour were the main things. Usually he just talked to the young people and their parents. He hardly ever had to take one of them to the station. In seven years he had only **arrested** five people. Yet in those seven years he had found eleven lost dogs, and returned them to their homes. Some policemen would have found that kind of life boring. But Michael was happy.

It was the middle of summer. The sun had just **set** and it was very late. Michael was at the police station. He was on the night **shift**. For a few hours he had been doing some paper-work. Even in a small village station there was a lot of **bureaucracy**. He had also had some coffee and had read the news-paper. The police station cat, Harriet, was sitting on his knee. She was **purring**.

"Sorry, Harriet," Michael said. "You're going to have to move. I want another coffee."

He tried to push the fat **tabby** cat off his lap, but she didn't want to go.

Suddenly the phone rang.

That's **strange**, Michael thought. Nobody ever called late at night unless something was really wrong.

He picked up the phone.

"Pendle Lee Police Station," he said.

"Oh, Michael," said a voice he **recognized**.

It was Mrs White, an **elderly** lady who lived on the edge of the village.

"I'm sorry it's so late," she said. "But there's something hap-pening in the **cemetery**."

to arrest	verhaften
to set	*hier*: unter-gehen
shift	Schicht(dienst)
bureaucracy	Bürokratie
to purr	schnurren
tabby	getigerte Katze
strange	seltsam
to recognize	erkennen
elderly	älter
cemetery	Friedhof

Michael **sighed**. Every now and again a group of teenagers would gather at the Pendle Lee Cemetery. Wearing black clothes, they would light candles and play loud music.
"Is it those kids again?" Michael asked.
"Maybe," Mrs White replied. "I can't sleep. And it **upsets me** that they go to the **graveyard**. My parents' and grandparents' **graves** are there."
"Of course," said Michael. "I'll go **right away**. Then maybe you can get some sleep."

to sigh	seufzen
to upset sb.	jmd. ärgern
graveyard	Friedhof
grave	Grab
right away	sofort
glow	Leuchten
to switch on	anschalten
torch	Taschenlampe
caretaker	Hausmeister
to glow	leuchten
to appear	auftauchen, erscheinen
to frighten sb.	jmd. erschrecken

Around ten minutes later, Michael parked the police car at the cemetery gates. He could hear music. The yellow **glow** of candles told him where the kids were. He got out of the car and **switched on** his **torch**. Next to the gates was a very old house. In the past the cemetery **caretaker** had lived in it. But the place had been standing empty for twenty years. Some of the windows were broken. Climbing plants had grown over the building. They had even gone through some of the windows.
Two hundred years ago, it had been really pretty. But now it looked like something from a scary movie. Nobody went inside. Birds had made their homes in the empty rooms.
Using his torch to light the way, Michael went towards the teenagers. Lots of candles were **glowing** on the graves. There was loud music, and some of the teenagers were standing in a circle singing.
When Michael **appeared** out of the darkness, he **frightened** some of them. A girl nearly screamed.

ghost	Gespenst
It's none of your business!	Das geht dich nichts an!
brave	mutig
fright	Schreck
Lancashire	engl. Grafschaft, benannt nach der Stadt Lancaster
devil	Teufel
to believe	glauben
magic spell	Zauberspruch
prison	Gefängnis
to hang sb.	jmd. erhängen
scapegoat	Sündenbock

"Sorry," he said to her. "It's only me. Are you trying to make a **ghost** appear?"

"**It's none of your business**," said a tall boy.

He stepped forward into the torchlight. Michael knew who he was. His name was Alex. He was seventeen years old, and his parents owned the bakery.

"It IS my business," Michael replied. "This is a cemetery. It's an important part of this community, and having a party here isn't respectful."

The girl who had nearly screamed came across to Michael.

"We can do what we want," she said. She was trying to sound **brave** after her **fright** earlier.

Michael recognized her now. Katie Lewis. She was only fourteen, and she should have been at home in bed.

"What are you doing?" Michael asked. "Are you trying to make contact with witches? I don't think you'll have any luck tonight."

Pendle Lee was in a part of **Lancashire** that was famous for its witches. In the early seventeenth century, some women and men from the area had been arrested. It was said that one talked to a black dog that was really the **devil**. The villagers believed that witches had made some people sick and even killed them. It was **believed** that cows stopped giving milk because of **magic spells**. The unlucky women and men were kept in **prison** at Lancaster Castle. The witches had been **hung** in 1612. Many people went to watch. Now the witches were seen as ordinary people who were **scapegoats** of the community. But the stories had continued until the present day. The Lancashire Witches brought many tourists to the area. People could buy toy witches. Lancaster Castle even had a special tour of the old prison rooms. And every year on Halloween, people from all over walked up Pendle Hill in the dark. Pendle Lee had its own stories, too. Some were about the cemetery. The first graves were over seven hundred years old. Long before the big Pendle Lee church was built, an even older church **existed** where the cemetery was. The stories told of witches meeting at the place where the old church once stood. It was said that they danced around large fires and tried to see the devil. The ghost of a witch called Agnes Cott was said to **haunt** the graveyard. Some people said that the caretaker's house was haunted, too. Strange noises were heard late at night. Strange lights were seen, too, even when the teenagers were in their beds.

Michael switched on his torch again.
"Time to go," he said to the kids, "before the ghost of Agnes Cott really does appear. Then you'll all run screaming back home anyway."
"You can't stop us," said Alex. "We'll come back again. The more this community hates us the happier we are."
"I'm sorry you feel that way," said Michael.
He did understand. There was nothing for teenagers to do in Pendle Lee. He thought that young people's discos at the **church hall** were a good idea. The villagers were worried about noise and alcohol. However, having teenagers on the streets at night was a bigger problem. After the kids left the graveyard, Michael looked around. There wasn't any graffiti on the graves

to exist	bestehen, existieren
to haunt	spuken (in)
church hall	Gemeindesaal

tonight. In the past there had been a problem with graffiti. Even some of the **headstones** had been **smashed**. That was a few years ago.
Alex and the other young people were angry and bored, but Michael didn't think they would do anything that bad. He decided to keep an eye on them anyway.

A few days later, Michael was on a normal afternoon shift. He liked to work during the day because there was more to do. He could walk around the village and talk to people. He could **stop by** the different shops and **chat** with the owners. At the station, other officers would come in from time to time. Even Harriet the cat liked the daytime best. On sunny days she could lie on the step outside the station. Anybody coming in or going out would have to step over her.
Mr Murphy, an elderly man, had called in at the station to give Michael some beans. Mr Murphy had grown them himself in his **allotment**. He was always stopping by with fresh vegetables. Like many older people, he used his allotment for pleasure rather than needing the food. He grew more than he could eat. Michael was just **admiring** the fresh green beans when his **mobile** rang.
"I'll just get that," Michael said to Mr Murphy.
He put the beans down. The call was from his boss, who had an office in the city.
"We've just heard from the Oswald Gallery," the Chief Inspector said. "They called the national **emergency** number. Can you go there, Michael? They've been **burgled**."

headstone	Grabstein
to smash	zerschlagen, zerschmettern
to stop by	vorbeischauen
to chat	plaudern
allotment	Schrebergarten
to admire	bewundern
mobile	Handy
emergency	Notfall
to burgle sth.	einbrechen in

Michael switched on the **sirens** as he drove quickly through the village in his car. As he drove, he thought about the gallery. He hadn't been there for over three years, but he used to go a lot. That was because his ex-girlfriend, Sarah, loved art. Sarah had left to go to America about three years ago. She worked in **art restoration**, and had been **offered** a job in Boston. After **thinking long and hard**, she decided to take it. But Michael couldn't get a job with the police in the United States. He didn't want to stop being a policeman either. So he stayed in Pendle Lee and Sarah moved to Boston.

siren	Sirene
art resto-ration	Gemälde-restaurierung
to offer	(an)bieten
to think long and hard	es sich reiflich überlegen
upset	erschrocken, aufgebracht
at once	*hier*: gleich-zeitig
Thank goodness!	Gott sei Dank!
to exclaim	ausrufen
fault	Fehler

The Oswald Gallery was just outside the village. It was in a beautiful eighteenth-century house. A man called John Oswald had built the house, and the gallery was named after him. It took Michael around ten minutes to get there. When he arrived, he walked to the door. Two elderly women quickly came to meet him. They looked **upset**. Both of them started speaking **at once**.

"Oh Sergeant,(i) **thank goodness** you're here!" one of the women **exclaimed**. "I'm Joan Potts. I work here."

"We don't know how it happened," the other lady was saying at the same time, "but it's my **fault**!"

Nur als direkte Anrede oder als Teil eines Namens werden Titel und Berufsbezeichnungen wie **Sergeant** im Englischen großgeschrieben. In allen anderen Fällen werden sie kleingeschrieben.

"No, Lottie, of course it's not your fault," said Joan.
"Yes it is!" Lottie exclaimed. "I'm so angry with myself!"

Michael raised his hands.
"Let's stay calm," he said. "We'll go inside and you can tell me all about it. Then we'll start searching for the **thief**."

thief	Dieb

Übung 1: Translation. Wie heißt das Wort auf Deutsch? Übersetzen Sie!

1. fields ______ Felder
2. village ______ Dorf
3. caring ______ mitfühlend
4. ancient ______ alt
5. cottage ______ Häuschen
6. happen ______ passieren / geschehen
7. gate ______ Tor
8. painting ______ ~~malen~~ Gemälde

Übung 2: Match-up. Welche Wörter passen zusammen? Ordnen Sie zu!

1. [e] elderly — a) shift night
2. [g] thank — b) spell magic
3. [f] stay — c) restoration
4. [c] art — d) caretaker — cemetery
5. [b] magic — e) man
6. [d] cemetery — f) calm night
7. [a] night — g) goodness

✓

Übung 3: Verb forms. Setzen Sie die Verben ins Simple Past!

1. arrive arrived
2. leave left
3. put put
4. hear heard
5. think thought

Übung 4: Choose the correct alternative. Kreuzen Sie die richtige Variante an!

1. The graveyard at night...
   - a) ☐ looked how something from a scary movie.
   - b) ☒ looked like something from a scary movie.
   - c) ☐ looked as something from a scary movie.
2. Police work involves...
   - a) ☐ much bureaucracies.
   - b) ☐ more bureaucracy.
   - c) ☒ a lot of bureaucracy.
3. He knew many people by name.
   - a) ☐ He called people names.
   - b) ☒ He knew lots of people quite well.
   - c) ☐ Many people knew his name.

2 Past Life

Once inside, Michael took out his notebook.
"Now tell me what happened," he said.
"No one had come to visit for over two hours," said Joan Potts. "It was a slow day."
Lottie Bingley sat down behind the **reception** desk.
"I'm afraid I left the reception," she said. "Every year we have a **competition** for artists. People from all over Lancashire send in their paintings. This morning we had some new paintings come in, and I was very excited. I wanted to see them, even though it's not my job to **unpack** them. I went upstairs to look. While I was gone, someone came in and **stole** one of our paintings. So it's all my fault."

reception	Empfang
competition	Wettbewerb
to unpack	auspacken
to steal	stehlen
security camera	Überwachungs-kamera

Michael looked all around the room.
"Don't you have **security cameras**?" he asked.
"No," Joan replied. "It would cost a lot of money. But we never imagined that someone would steal from the Oswald Gallery!"
"And neither of you saw anybody?" Michael asked.
"No." Both women replied at the same time.
"We didn't see or hear anything," said Lottie.
"Let's have a look at where the painting was hung," Michael said.
The women led him into one of the gallery's little rooms. Modern galleries had lots of space and white paint, but the

hall	Flur
crime scene	Tatort
fingerprint	Fingerabdruck
investigation	Ermittlung
background	Hintergrund

Oswald Gallery was different. The building had many small rooms and **halls**. The walls were covered in beautiful old wood. The windows were very small. As visitors walked around, they could imagine living three hundred years ago. Paintings were hung on all the walls, but in one place there was an empty spot.

"It was here," said Joan. "It was called 'Summer'."

Michael took out his phone.

"I'm going to call the **crime scene** police," he told Joan and Lottie. "Someone will come round and check for **fingerprints**. I'll also need a photograph of the painting, please. It'll help in the **investigation**."

"I'll go and find one," said Lottie. "The artist was Butterworth, of course."

The Oswald Gallery was small and not very important. But it had the largest collection of Butterworth paintings in the country. Tristan Butterworth was a famous painter from the 1940s and 50s. He had lived near Pendle Lee for many years. When he died in the 1980s, many of his best paintings were given to the gallery. People came from all over the United Kingdom to see them.

Lottie came back into the reception and handed a large photograph to Michael.

"Here it is," she said. "'Summer'. It's a wonderful picture, isn't it?"

Michael looked at it. It showed a beautiful summer scene. In the **background** the sun shone on a river. Green fields and trees were all around. In the front of the painting there was a large tree, and under it sat a young woman. She was wearing

database	Datenbank
to alert sb.	jmd. alarmieren, warnen
burglary	Einbruch (-diebstahl)

an old-fashioned yellow dress and a big hat.
"This was painted in 1951," Lottie said. "Looking at it makes me feel so calm. It almost feels like you're really there."
"It's lovely," said Michael. "I'll need to keep this photograph for our investigation. Is that okay?"
"Of course," said Lottie. "We'll do whatever we can to help."

Back inside his car, Michael phoned his boss, Chief Inspector Blake. He gave Blake all the information he had so far. The inspector was very busy. Michael could tell he wasn't very interested in a painting stolen from a village gallery. The city had more crime than the police could deal with.
"They should have had security cameras," Blake said angrily.
He told Michael to contact the Art Loss Register. It kept an international **database** of art that had been stolen or lost. If a rich person or a museum wanted to buy a piece of art, they could find out if it was stolen through the Register. If it was, the buyer could **alert** the police. The thief who was trying to sell the art could then be caught.
It was hard to find stolen art. Sometimes the buyer knew it was stolen, but didn't care. Sometimes a group of thieves would plan a big **burglary**, and then wait for many years before selling the art in places like Africa or South America.
"Can you deal with this?" Blake asked Michael. "I don't have another officer who can come down there right now. It's too bad we have to send you a crime scene officer just to take some fingerprints."
"I still think it's a good idea," Michael said.
The inspector was often in a bad mood, and Michael was glad he didn't have to work in the city with him.

terror alert	Terroralarm
wavy	gewellt
to wonder	sich fragen
imagination	Vorstellung
to interview	befragen, verhören
meanwhile	währenddessen
to explore	erkunden
to match with	*hier*: passen zu
Crimestoppers number	Telefonnummer für sachdienliche Hinweise

"You know we're on **terror alert**, don't you?" Blake went on. "We may have to send officers to Manchester or London at any moment. You too, Sergeant."

"I know," Michael replied. "Leave everything to me, Inspector. I'll send you my reports."

After the phone call was finished, Michael opened the car window. He took a deep breath of fresh air. Then he looked at the photograph of 'Summer' again. The young woman in the picture was very pretty. She had long, **wavy** blonde hair. She looked out across the fields. Michael **wondered** if the woman had been real, or if she had come from the painter's **imagination**.

Michael was soon back at the station. He immediately contacted the Art Loss Register. He informed them about the stolen painting and gave all the details. Then he went out and **interviewed** the villagers. He was hoping someone had seen something strange, like someone hurrying away from the village. **Meanwhile** the crime scene officer was **exploring** the gallery. If fingerprints were found, they would be put into the police fingerprint database. If the thief had done anything wrong before, his (or her) prints would be in the database. They would **match with** the prints from the crime scene. Then the police would have a name.

Over the next two days, Michael was busy. He put up signs about the burglary. The signs asked people with any information to call the police or the national **Crimestoppers number**.

He also went from house to house, asking the villagers if they had seen a stranger in the village. A few couples and families had had picnics or had stopped at the White Witch pub. But nobody had been behaving strangely. He made copies of the 'Summer' photograph. Then he took them to all the art shops and auction houses in the area. He sent the photo to colleagues in Preston, Manchester, and even London.
At the station he put the photo on the wall. Instead of trying to find a stolen painting, he began to feel that he was trying to find the beautiful woman. It seemed very important to take her back to the gallery where she lived.

stranger	Fremder
unconscious	bewusstlos

After a few days, the other police officers started to joke about Michael's painting. He looked at it a hundred times a day. Sometimes, when he was talking to someone, his eyes would go to the photograph.
"Have you fallen in love?" some of the officers asked.
Michael no longer chatted with the villagers. He didn't seem to have time any more. Even Harriet the cat seemed in a bad mood because of 'Summer'. Michael only wanted to hunt for the painting, and was no longer interested in playing with her. Whenever he had a moment, he was on the phone or visiting auction houses, asking about the painting. Even when he was not at work, he'd visit places that sold old paintings.
On Tuesday afternoon, the phone rang. It was exactly five days since 'Summer' had been stolen. Every time the phone rang, Michael hoped it was about the painting. It was Joan Potts from the gallery.
"Something terrible has happened!" she exclaimed. "Lottie has been taken to hospital. Another painting was stolen and this time, the thief pushed Lottie down the stairs. She's unconscious."

After going **straight** to the gallery and looking at the crime scene, Michael went to the hospital with Joan. They were both very worried about Lottie. Because she was old, her chances of getting better quickly were not good. She'd hit her head quite badly, and broken one of her legs.

Joan couldn't help crying as they stood in the waiting room at the hospital. The doctor **in charge** promised to call Michael as soon as there was a change. Michael needed to ask her about what happened. Perhaps Lottie saw the thief coming up the stairs. But while she was unconscious and in danger, all he could do was wait and hope.

straight	direkt, geradewegs
in charge	verantwortlich, zuständig
landscape	Landschaft
still-life	Stillleben
clue	Hinweis, Spur

Meanwhile, he needed to contact the Art Loss Register about the second stolen painting. It was another Butterworth, called 'Evening in June'. This time it was of a terrace outside a lovely old house. There was a table with teacups and a teapot, and a large strawberry cake. On one of the chairs sat a woman. Michael recognized her as the woman from 'Summer'. This time she was dressed in a pretty purple dress. She was reading a book. In the background were green hills and the sun was just going down. The sunset seemed to make the picture glow.

Michael thought it was strange that both paintings were of the same woman. There were many Butterworth pictures that showed **landscapes** or **still-life** scenes. Only a few had the young woman in them. Perhaps that was a **clue**.

"Who was she?" Michael asked when he called Joan that night.

"Don't you know?" asked Joan. "It's Sylvia. Sylvia and Tristan Butterworth got married in 1950. She was very beautiful and was his model for some of his paintings."

"Maybe if we find out more about Sylvia Butterworth, it might give us a clue," Michael said. "Perhaps the thief wants to collect paintings of her."
"Good idea," said Joan. "Maybe he's **obsessed with** her. We have an **archive** at the gallery. It has a lot of information about Sylvia in it. You can look at it if you like."

The next day, after his afternoon shift, Michael went back to the Oswald Gallery. It had been closed, and there were plans to buy security cameras. The risk of someone getting **hurt** again was too big. Joan took Michael upstairs to a small office. It was filled with **filing cabinets**.

obsessed (with)	besessen (von)
archive	Archiv
to hurt	verletzen; schmerzen
filing cabinet	Aktenschrank
exhibition	Ausstellung
reason	Grund
file	Akte

"This is the Butterworth archive," Joan said. "The filing cabinets are full of photographs and letters. They belonged to both Tristan and Sylvia. There are also lots of papers about Butterworth's paintings and **exhibitions**. You can look through them, if you like."
Joan made him a cup of coffee. Then she gave him the keys to the gallery and the code number of the alarm system. She went back to the hospital, where she spent her evenings sitting with Lottie. Michael was alone. He didn't know where to start looking. All he knew was that someone had a **reason** for stealing Butterworth's paintings of Sylvia. Perhaps the past would give him a clue.
First he pulled open some **files** of photographs. There were lots of black-and-white ones. There were many of Sylvia by herself. Michael knew they were not important for the investigation, but he couldn't help looking. Some were of Sylvia

when she was very young. Most showed her in her twenties and thirties.
Michael felt that he had never seen anyone more beautiful. Sylvia had big, dark eyes and a glowing smile. She was quite tall and looked strong and **confident**. When she was younger, she had worn her long hair **down**. When she was older, she wore it up, in the style of the 1950s. Her clothes were always pretty and looked good on her. In some of the photos, she was with a man. Michael recognized him as Tristan Butterworth. The names, places and dates were written on the backs of many photos.
There were many pictures, for example, of Tristan and Sylvia in a **gorgeous** landscape. In the background were lakes and mountains. On the backs of the pictures were the words '**Honeymoon**, Cumbria, 1950'. The couple looked very happy. Some of the photographs showed other people, too.
There were many that had been taken on the terrace of a house. Michael thought it was the same terrace as in 'Evening in June'. In the photos lots of people were standing around. They had glasses of wine and cigarettes. In other photos the same people were sitting under a tree, having a picnic. Behind them the Pendle Lee river flowed. Everyone was smiling at the camera. There were a few pictures of Butterworth with another man. The pictures said 'Nigel and Tristan', with different places and dates. There were also pictures of 'Nigel and Sylvia'.
Next he looked at some old letters. There were lots from Sylvia to Tristan. Michael began to read. He read for a long time. When he looked at his watch, he had been reading for over an hour. He had been in a different world. It seemed as though

confident	selbstsicher
down	*hier*: offen, lose
gorgeous	herrlich, wunderschön
honeymoon	Flitterwochen

Sylvia was writing to him. He put down the letters and picked up some different ones. All of them were to Sylvia from a man named Nigel Huxley. Some were dated from 1941 to 1944, and had been sent from France.

Michael looked through them quickly. Huxley had written about being a **soldier** in World War II. He wrote about being frightened when bombs fell close by. He also told her about other soldiers, who had died. Some of the letters were very **serious**. But others were full of fun. In these light letters, he wrote about parties and friends. Huxley had written 'To my darling Sylvia' at the top of the letters. It was clear that he had been in love with her. Michael took out his notebook and wrote down Nigel's name. Perhaps he was still alive. Maybe he had more information about Sylvia and the paintings.

soldier	Soldat
serious	ernst

Michael had been in the archive for hours. At last he decided to go home. He wanted to come back as soon as possible, because there were many more letters and papers to look at. But before he left, Michael opened the filing cabinet with the photos. There was one he wanted to see again. The photo showed Sylvia sitting on a beach. She was wearing a big sun hat and a white dress. Her hair was down. In her hands was a small book. She had stopped reading and was looking into the camera. But instead of smiling, Sylvia looked serious. Michael felt that she was looking right at him. Before he could stop himself, he had picked up the photo.

Then he put it into his pocket. He had never stolen anything in his life. Now he was a thief, just like the person who had taken the paintings.

Michael had spent many hours in the archive, and it was now night-time. On his way home, he drove past the cemetery. He was worried that the teenagers were there again. Suddenly, he saw something. It looked like the glow from a candle or a torch. It seemed to be moving **among** the graves.

"Those kids!" Michael said out loud.

He looked at his watch: 12:16 a.m.

Michael stopped the car at the gates and got out his torch. Then he went into the cemetery. The light seemed to have **disappeared**. He listened, but he couldn't hear anything. The moon was shining brightly, and the air smelled like cut grass and old flowers. He walked on. The graves looked quite scary in the dark. Although he didn't believe in ghosts, Michael didn't feel very brave. It was like a graveyard scene from a scary movie.

among	zwischen
to disappear	verschwinden
to hide	(sich) verstecken
to be about to do sth.	im Begriff sein, etw. zu tun

Suddenly he got angry. The teenagers were probably **hiding** from him. Maybe Alex and his friends were all sitting behind the headstones, waiting for him to go away. They probably thought this was funny. Michael decided to switch off his torch (i) and wait for the kids to come out.

The moonlight helped him to see quite well. But suddenly a cloud moved across the sky and the moonlight disappeared. It was very dark. Michael turned around in a circle. Nothing. No light. And he still couldn't hear anything, either.

He **was about to** switch his torch back on when he saw a small light. It was near the old caretaker's house. There was someone there. Michael put

Bei vielen **Phrasal Verbs** kann das Objekt sowohl vor als auch nach der Präposition stehen:
He switched his torch off.
Ein Objektpronomen steht aber immer vor der Präposition:
He switched it off.

on his torch again. He shone it across the graves towards the empty old house.

"Hello!" he called out.

Immediately the candlelight disappeared. Michael started to walk.

apart from	außer
spider's web	Spinnennetz

"It's Sergeant Rose here. What are you doing?"

When he reached the house, he shone his torch all around. There was nobody there. However, a strange symbol had appeared on the front door. It showed three stars inside a circle, painted in yellow paint. He tried the door, but it wouldn't open. He went up to some of the windows and shone his torch inside. The rooms were empty **apart from** some broken tables and chairs. There were **spider's webs** everywhere.

"Whoever you are," Michael said to the empty air, "you should go home."

Suddenly he heard a ghostly laugh. He couldn't tell if it was a man's or a woman's voice. Before he could turn around, there was a sharp pain in his head, and he was falling towards the ground.

Übung 5: Question words. Setzen Sie die richtigen Fragepronomen ein!

which | who | where | why | what | when

1. where was the painting hung?
2. what kind of competition was it?
3. when does the gallery open?
4. which of the paintings was stolen?
5. why were Joan and Lottie so upset?
6. who works at the gallery?

Übung 6: Odd one out. Welches Wort passt nicht in die Reihe? Finden Sie das „schwarze Schaf"!

1. paint | cook | photograph | draw
2. moonlight | torchlight | sunlight | starlight
3. pretty | strange | weird | bizarre
4. ghost | witch | vampire | murderer
5. steal | rob | burgle | sell
6. box | circle | triangle | square
7. graveyard | museum | headstone | cemetery
8. torch | candle | soldier | lamp
9. clue | confident | obsessed | frightened

Übung 7: Opposites. Finden Sie das passende Gegenteil!

1. e few	a) strange
2. c push	b) quiet
3. f wrong	c) pull
4. h friendly	d) ugly
5. a normal	e) many
6. g slow	f) right
7. i daytime	g) fast
8. d beautiful	h) unfriendly
9. b loud	i) night-time

3 Young Woman with Flowers

When Michael finally opened his eyes, his clothes were wet from lying in the grass for a long time. He put his hand to his head. When he looked at his hand, there was something dark on his fingers. Blood. He felt sick and his head hurt. His torch was lying on the ground, but it wasn't working any more. Michael looked around. He didn't know what to do. The best thing would be to call his boss, then go to the hospital and get a doctor to look at him. He stood up. All he wanted to do was get into bed. Slowly, he went back to his car and drove home.

Early the next morning, Michael went to the station. He wrote a report about what happened in the graveyard. His head still hurt badly, but he didn't want to spend the day waiting to see a doctor. Instead he called the hospital about Lottie. She was still unconscious, and the doctors were doing all sorts of tests. After the hospital call, he phoned the homes of Alex and some of the other teenagers from the cemetery. He asked their parents to bring them down to the station as soon as possible. If Alex had hit Michael, he was in serious trouble. Then he arranged for another officer to talk to the teenagers. Although Michael wanted to talk to Alex and the others himself, he was a **witness** to a crime. He couldn't be the questioning officer, too. Then Michael searched the Internet for Nigel Huxley. Huxley might have information about the paintings or Sylvia. He found out that Huxley had also been an artist. He was a **sculptor**,

witness	Zeuge
sculptor	Bildhauer

but he was not as famous as Butterworth. His last sculpture was made in 1967. Now Huxley lived in a village only 20 kilometres from Pendle Lee. He was 85 years old, and it seemed that he was very rich.

nearby	in der Nähe
to pay sb. a visit	jmd. einen Besuch abstatten
mansion	Villa, Herrenhaus
housekeeper	Haushälterin

Michael thought about everything he now knew about Huxley. He lived nearby and knew about art. And although he was old, you didn't have to be fit to push an old lady downstairs. He had been in love with Sylvia. Perhaps he had driven to the gallery. He could have stolen 'Summer' while Lottie was looking at the new paintings upstairs. The second time, Lottie may have seen him stealing 'Evening in June'. He might have pushed her down the stairs, then put the painting in the car and driven home.

Michael decided to pay Huxley a visit.

But first he put out some cat food for Harriet. The big tabby was still in a bad mood. Michael just wanted to talk about, think about and dream about those paintings! He had no time for cats or the other villagers. When Mr Murphy came in that morning with a bag of aubergines, Michael had simply thanked him and looked back at the computer.

At lunch time, Michael drove to the nearby village. It took him a long time to find Huxley's house. The house was very large. In fact, it was a mansion, but it was hidden behind lots of trees on the edge of the village. Michael parked the police car in front of the house. It was a lovely old place. There were lots of steps leading to a big door. Michael went up and rang the bell. After a few moments, an elderly woman opened the door.

"Mrs Huxley?" Michael asked.

"No, I'm the housekeeper," the woman said.

to point to	zeigen auf
fireplace	(offener) Kamin

She looked at his police uniform and car. For some reason, she didn't seem too happy.

"Do you want to see Mr Huxley?"

"Yes, please, if he's at home," Michael replied.

"You'd better come in," said the housekeeper.

Michael followed her into the house.

"Wait here." The housekeeper **pointed to** a chair by the door. She wasn't friendly at all. Michael wondered if she ever smiled. He sat down. The big hall was painted a light green. The floor was made of gorgeous dark wood. In the corner stood a large sculpture. Michael couldn't really tell what it was. It could have been a woman with long wavy hair. Or a tree. Whatever it was, it looked very modern.

Suddenly the housekeeper appeared again.

"You can see Mr Huxley now," she said. "He's in the living room."

Nigel Huxley sat in a big chair. He didn't look 85 at all. He seemed a lot younger. But perhaps that was because of his bright blue eyes. He looked intelligent and full of energy.

"I'm sorry about my housekeeper," Huxley said. "She's not very nice to visitors, even policemen."

Michael looked around the living room. The sun was shining through the large windows. There were two huge sofas and a few chairs. In the middle of the room was a round table. Lots of books were everywhere: on the table, on bookshelves and on the floor. There was also a beautiful old **fireplace**. Above the fireplace, on the wall, there was a painting. Michael immediately recognized Sylvia.

"That's a Butterworth picture!" he exclaimed.

"Yes," Huxley said. "It's called 'Young Woman with Flowers'. Tristan Butterworth gave it to me."

robbery	Raubüberfall
badly	*hier*: sehr, unbedingt
detective work	Ermittlungsarbeit

The painting showed Sylvia holding lots of flowers. They were pink, orange and red. The background was a dark green, and Sylvia was wearing a green dress.

Michael couldn't take his eyes off the picture. Even when the housekeeper came in with tea and biscuits, he couldn't stop looking at Sylvia.

"How can I help you?" Huxley asked, taking a cup of tea and a chocolate biscuit.

Michael finally took his eyes off the painting and looked at the old man.

"I'm sorry, Mr Huxley, I should have introduced myself. I'm Sergeant Rose from the police station at Pendle Lee. You heard about the **robbery** at the gallery?" asked Michael.

"Of course," Huxley replied. "I collect Butterworth paintings. I'm often at the Oswald Gallery."

"You know that Lottie Bingley is unconscious in hospital?" Michael asked, watching Huxley closely.

"Yes. It's very sad and upsetting," Huxley said.

Michael looked at the picture of Sylvia above the fireplace.

"Somebody wanted those pictures very **badly**," he said. "Badly enough to almost kill an elderly woman. Both paintings were of Sylvia. I think we should look for someone who is obsessed with her."

Huxley's eyes shone and he gave a small smile.

"So you've come to question me," he said. "Good **detective work**, Sergeant Rose. It's true, I was in love with Sylvia. She and I grew up together. Our families were friends. We lived in the same village and went to the same church. Even when I was a teenager, I loved her. I met Tristan Butterworth at art school. Sylvia would model for us both. Then the Second

memory	Erinnerung
to break the law	das Gesetz brechen
to disappoint sb.	jmd. enttäuschen
search warrant	Durchsuchungsbefehl

World War started. I became a soldier, but Tristan couldn't join the army. He had polio when he was a baby and there was something wrong with his leg. While I was in France, Tristan and Sylvia fell in love. I wanted them to be happy, so we stayed friends."

"What happened to Tristan and Sylvia?" Michael asked. He'd almost forgotten about the stolen art.

"The Butterworths moved to America in the 1960s," Huxley went on. "We wrote letters at Christmas, but after a few years our letters stopped. I heard they were living in New York. Tristan had an exhibition at the Museum of Modern Art. Then I read in the paper that he had died in 1986. I never saw Sylvia again. I tried to find her, but with no luck. Now my paintings of Sylvia bring back wonderful **memories** of summer."

"Would you **break the law** to get more of those memories?" Michael asked.

"I'm sorry to **disappoint** you," said Huxley, "but I didn't steal those paintings."

"So you won't **mind** if I look around your house?" Michael asked.

"Yes, I do mind, Sergeant Rose," the old man replied, standing up. "My house is private. If you don't have a **search warrant**, please leave."

Huxley was starting to get angry. But Michael knew he was right. Without a search warrant, the police couldn't search someone's home. Michael had to leave. He thanked Huxley for his time.

On his way out to the car again, he thought about the old man. Firstly, he seemed obsessed with Sylvia and collected paintings of her. Secondly, he was familiar with the Oswald

Gallery and lived close by. Thirdly, he didn't want the police looking around his house.

Michael decided to call Chief Inspector Blake to find out if he could get a search warrant for the mansion.

wallet	Geldbeutel
security	Sicherheit
confused	verwirrt
relieved	erleichtert

Later that night, Michael decided to go to the gallery. He wanted to look in the archives again, and still had the key. He wasn't really thinking about the investigation. He was wondering if Sylvia was still alive in New York or somewhere else. She would be an old woman by now. In his imagination, however, she was a beautiful young woman. He wanted her to stay that way. He still kept the photo of Sylvia in his **wallet**. Every now and then, he took it out and looked at it. Before he left for the gallery, he called Joan Potts. He wanted to let her know that he would visit the archive.

Now that the gallery was closed, she believed the paintings would be safe. However, she was still happy to know that a policeman was around. She also told him that they had bought a new **security** system. There were cameras for every room. In two days' time[i] it would be installed. Then they could open the gallery again. Meanwhile, Lottie was out of danger. She could open her eyes and talk a little bit. She had no memories at all of the robbery. She was **confused** about being in the hospital. Still, Michael was **relieved** that she was getting better.

Statt in **two days' time** kann man auch einfach **in two days** sagen. Beides bedeutet „in zwei Tagen". Die Wendung in ... days' time hebt aber die Zeitspanne, die vergeht, etwas mehr hervor.

6

Übung 8: True or false. Kreuzen Sie die richtigen Aussagen an!

1. Nigel Huxley is 75 years old. ☐
2. Huxley had been in love with Sylvia. ☒
3. Michael thinks that Huxley might have pushed Lottie down the stairs. ☒
4. Huxley allows Michael to search his house. ☐
5. After the Second World War, Huxley lost contact to Sylvia and Tristan Butterworth. ☒
6. Michael kept a photo of Sylvia in his wallet. ☒

Übung 9: Translation quiz. Übersetzen Sie und enträtseln Sie das Lösungswort!

1. Villa MANSION
2. Taschenlampe TORCH
3. Erinnerung MEMORY
4. Geldbeutel WALLET POCKET
5. Friedhof CEMETERY
6. selbstsicher CONFIDENT

Lösung: STOLEN

Übung 10: Choose the correct alternative. Wählen Sie die richtige Variante!

1. He wasn't really though / thinking about the investigation.
2. It taked / took him a long time to find Huxley's house.
3. He was wondering / wandering if Sylvia was still alive.
4. He didn't know / now what to do.
5. Michael couldn't take his eyes of / off the picture.
6. He looked at the picture of Sylvia above / about the fireplace.

above

4 Voices in the Dark

By the time Michael got to the Oswald Gallery, the sun had nearly disappeared. He parked his car right in front of the door, and was **shocked** about what he saw. There was graffiti all over the front of the building. It was the same yellow paint that he'd seen at the caretaker's house, and the same symbols. Then he saw the broken window. The hole was big enough for someone to climb through, but bits of glass were still sharp. The robber had probably been hurt. Michael looked through the broken window. A big rock from the garden was lying inside, on the wooden floor. Bits of broken glass were everywhere. On one piece of glass he saw something red. It looked like blood. The thief had been cut. This meant that the police could get an important DNA clue. Michael immediately took out his mobile phone. He called the city station. Another officer would come to Pendle Lee as soon as possible. The crime scene officer would come, too.

shocked	schockiert

Michael didn't want to stand outside waiting. He decided to go in. Perhaps the thief was still in the gallery. Trying to stay calm, he opened the front door. Then he stopped and listened. He couldn't hear anything. He took another step. The wooden floor made a loud noise. Then, slowly and quietly, he went to the room with the broken window. There were paintings on the wall. Some of them were landscapes from the Butterworth collection. There were also sculptures. But Michael was more interested in the blood. It was a very dark red because it was

trail	Spur
to greet sb.	jmd. grüßen
constable	Wachtmeister, Polizist
match	*hier*: Treffer

almost dry. It made a small **trail** across the floor and into the hall. Michael followed it. The trail went up the stairs, along the hall, and into another room. It stopped in front of a wall. There was an empty space where a painting once hung.

Suddenly, there was a shout from downstairs. The two other policemen had arrived. Michael went downstairs and **greeted** them. He told them about the trail of blood and the stolen painting.

"Can you go through the rest of the building?" he asked the **constable**, whose name was John Ritchie. "I'm going to look in the garden."

"I'll get fingerprints and blood," said the crime scene officer. "But I don't think we'll get a **match**. There were no matches on our fingerprint database last time."

Just as Michael was about to go outside, the constable called him back.

"You're the one who was hit in the graveyard, aren't you?" he asked. "I talked to those teenagers. Every single one has an alibi. Even Alex, who is an angry young man. One day he'll end up arrested for something, believe me!"

Michael thanked him, then took his torch and went outside. There was no moonlight, so it was very dark. He walked all around the building, looking and listening. On one side of the garden was the car park. Two police cars were parked there. On the other side of the garden there were woods. They made a good hiding place. Michael went into the trees. It was very dark, almost black. The trees looked very tall in the white light from the torch. Michael thought about his visits to the cemetery. Now he was walking through woods at night. His torch had become his best friend. It was a good thing he did not believe in ghosts or witches. If they were real, he would have seen one by now. In fact, he felt like the ghost of Pendle Lee himself. That's what happened when you spent too much time in graveyards and dark places.

Suddenly, he heard a noise. He immediately stopped walking and listened. He wondered if it was a small animal making noises in the dark. But then he heard a voice. Another voice answered. Two people were hiding in the woods. Michael took out his phone and called PC Ritchie. He spoke very quietly and quickly. The constable agreed to join him.

In less than a minute the constable was there, walking softly through the trees. Then they both switched off their torches. After a few moments, their eyes could see better in the darkness. They quietly walked towards the sound of voices. Two people were hiding in some bushes underneath a tree. They were dressed all in black, and had long black hair. This just made their white faces stand out even more in the dark. Michael recognized two young men from the cemetery. He gave a shout. The boys looked around and saw the officers, then jumped up and started to run. Michael and PC Ritchie raced after them through the trees. The teenagers were fast, but frightened. They kept looking behind them. Suddenly one of them hit a tree and fell to the ground.

PC (Police Constable)	Wachtmeister
to manage to do sth.	es schaffen, etw. zu tun

"It's a good idea to look where you're going," said Michael as he pulled the boy to his feet.

Meanwhile, PC Ritchie had **managed to** stop the other one. The constable took the boy's rucksack and opened it. He shone his torch inside.

"What do we have here, boys?" PC Ritchie asked, shining his light on cans of yellow spray paint.

spray paint	Sprühfarbe
involved in	beteiligt an
insulting	beleidigend

At the police station, Michael and PC Ritchie questioned the teenagers. They said they'd painted the symbols on the walls, but had had nothing to do with the smashed window or the burglary. Just after doing the graffiti, they'd heard someone walking through the car park. They'd gone into the woods, and then heard the sound of breaking glass. One of the boys' fathers was in the room with them, which was normal when a 15-year-old was involved in a crime.

"Why didn't you call the police?" he asked his son.

"I hate the pigs," said the boy, using the insulting word for policemen. "Can we go now?"

The police would wait until daylight to search the woods for the stolen painting. Michael didn't want to let the boys go until then, but he had to. There was no reason for arresting them. They were checked for cuts, because of the broken glass in the gallery window. But neither of the boys had been cut anywhere on their bodies.

They were in lots of trouble about the graffiti, but Michael didn't think anything serious would happen to them. He let them go home with their parents.

Back at his desk, he made some notes for his report. Then he made a list of things to do in the morning. At the top was the search warrant for Nigel Huxley's home. He wanted to visit the old sculptor as soon as possible. He wanted to have some of Huxley's blood for testing, too. The investigators could match it against the blood from the gallery. Next, he wanted to take Joan Potts to the gallery to ask her about the stolen painting.

to yell	(laut) schreien
dare	Mutprobe

He was sure it was another one of Sylvia. Then, he wanted to go to the hospital to see if Lottie had any memories of the robbery. Suddenly, the phone rang. Michael picked it up.

"Hello?" he said.

"Michael, it's Mrs White," said the woman on the phone. "Sorry I'm calling so late. It's those kids in the cemetery."

"Not again." Michael sighed.

He was disappointed. There were bigger things than bad behaviour going on in Pendle Lee.

"I'll go immediately," he said. It wasn't illegal to be at a cemetery at night, but it wasn't respectful.

"Perhaps we can ask the ghost of Agnes Cott to give them a fright," Mrs White said. "Then they'll stay at home every night!"

Michael gave a short laugh.

"I'll ask her to pay them a visit," he said.

Once more, Michael drove to the cemetery. Once more, he parked at the gates and got out his torch. There were candles glowing among the graves. He could see young people sitting around. Loud music was playing. He recognized the tall figure of Alex. When he got close to the group, Alex saw him and stood up. The young man looked angry. Michael felt angry, too, but he didn't want to get involved in a fight with teenagers.

"Go away!" Alex **yelled**.

Michael was just about to reply when he heard a loud scream. It sounded like it was coming from the caretaker's cottage. Immediately Michael started to run to the old house. Alex ran, too.

"It's Katie!" Alex exclaimed. "She went into the house for a **dare**."

to rush	eilen, sich beeilen
to be on fire	brennen, in Flammen stehen

"Can't you kids stay out of trouble?" Michael shouted as he ran.
When he got to the house, he tried to open the door. It was still locked.
"She went through a window," said Alex.
Together they ran to the side of the building. Just then, Katie screamed again. Michael found the window. It was old-fashioned, and the old wood had made it easy to open from the outside. He shone his torch inside and called Katie's name. He saw her rush into the room, looking very frightened. When she saw Michael and Alex, she started to cry and immediately tried to climb through the window. Michael helped her.
Once outside, Katie fell on the ground. She lay on the grass.
"It's the witch!" she said. She couldn't stop crying.
"What did she look like?" Alex asked.
Michael looked at the young man angrily. "There are no witches," he said. "Or ghosts."
Then he saw a strange glow coming from inside the house. It was very bright orange.
Katie and Alex saw it, too.
"I dropped my candle," said Katie.
The old house was on fire.
Michael immediately pulled his mobile phone from his pocket. He called the emergency number. But just as he was about to speak, he saw a figure inside the house.
"There's someone in there!" he exclaimed.
"The witch!" Katie cried. "I told you. She's real!"
Michael threw the mobile to Alex, who immediately told the emergency services where they were. Then Michael climbed through the broken window into the burning house.
"Police!" he called out, but the figure had disappeared.

burning	brennend
to choke	ersticken, würgen
old people's home	Seniorenheim
to remember sth.	sich erinnern an

He ran through the room and into the hall. Spider's webs were on his face and in his hair. The fire seemed to come from the front room. He could feel how hot it was. He was choking on heavy smoke. He looked around, confused. Then he saw her: a woman was going up the stairs. He had no time. The fire was going to burn the old building down. He ran up the stairs. He could see quite well because of the orange glow from the fire. When he got to the top, he saw her standing very still, looking at him. For a moment, he thought that Katie was right. The woman was a witch.

Agnes Cott, he thought. She had long grey hair and dirty old clothes. She looked very old. Michael told her his name.

"I'm here to help you," he said.

She turned and ran down the corridor.

Michael followed her. He could see smoke from the fire coming up the stairs. He went into one of the bedrooms. Although it was darker in the room, he could see the old woman. She was trying to pick up some large, flat objects. When Michael got closer, he saw that the objects were paintings. On every one, he recognized Sylvia. The old woman looked at Michael and started to cry.

"Please help me!" she said.

Two months later, after his evening shift, Michael left the station. He walked up the road. When he got to the old people's home, he stopped. Nigel Huxley was waiting for him. It was the same every Wednesday and Sunday. The two men went inside together.

Sometimes Sylvia couldn't remember[i] their names. She

couldn't remember pushing Lottie down the stairs, or laughing and knocking Michael out in the graveyard. For weeks she'd been living in the old caretaker's cottage. She stole things to eat, as well as the paintings. She couldn't be put in prison for her crimes because she had Alzheimer's disease. Instead, at the old people's home she had food, clothing and good care. She mainly remembered things that happened sixty years ago.

disease	Krankheit
care	Pflege, Betreuung

Michael knew she had been beautiful then, although he couldn't tell from looking at the old woman now. He and Nigel would listen to her stories about wonderful summer evenings, and her eyes would glow with happiness.

"Her eyes are the one thing that hasn't changed," Michael said to Nigel, looking at the photo of Sylvia in his wallet. "They're still beautiful."

Achten Sie immer auf den Unterschied zwischen **remind** und **remember**!
to remember sth.
= sich erinnern an
to remind sb. of sth.
= jmd. an etw. erinnern

Übung 11: Personal pronouns. Ersetzen Sie die hervorgehobenen Personen durch die richtigen Pronomen!

1. **Lottie** *She* was pushed down the stairs.
2. **Two policemen** they were helping with the investigation.
3. **You and I** we don't know who the thief is.
4. **Michael** he followed the trail of blood upstairs.
5. Michael told **Lottie and Joan** them to get cameras.
6. Can you tell **my friend and I** us where the gallery is?
7. We will visit **Lottie** her in the hospital.
8. Tell **Michael** him about the stolen painting!
9. "I'm here to help **the woman** ~~her~~ you," Michael told her.
10. "Don't you have security cameras?" he asked **Lottie and Joan**.

Übung 12: Unscramble the sentences. Bringen Sie die Wörter in die richtige Reihenfolge und bilden Sie sinnvolle Sätze!

1. their Sylvia remember sometimes couldn't names

   Sometimes Sylvia couldn't remember their names ✓

2. thing eyes are one that her hasn't the changed

   Her eyes are one thing that hasn't changed.

   ~~*One thing hasn't changed that are her eyes.*~~

3. into through the the Michael house window burning climbed broken

   Michael climbed through the broken window into the burning house ✓

4. anywhere neither cut of boys had the been

   (on) their bodies

   ~~*Neither anywhere had been*~~

   of the boys had been cut anywhere on their bodies

5. gallery perhaps still thief in the the was

   Perhaps the thief was still in the gallery ✓

Übung 13: Plurals. Geben Sie die Pluralform an!

1. thief ~~thiefs~~ thieves
2. woman women
3. gallery ~~gallerys~~ galleries
4. information ~~informations~~
5. memory memories
6. noise noises
7. system systems
8. witch witches

Abschlusstest

Übung 1: Verb forms. Setzen Sie die richtige Verbfom ein!

1. After the phone call was finished, Michael open opened the car window.
2. He saw her rush rush into the room, looking very frightened.
3. Two people hide were hiding ~~hided~~ in some bushes underneath a tree.
4. Tomorrow, someone come will come round and check for fingerprints.
5. In the picture, Sylvia wear was wearing a big sun hat and a white dress.

Übung 2: Questions to the text. Beantworten Sie die Fragen zum Text in ganzen Sätzen!

1. Who stole the Butterworth paintings and why?

Sylvia stole the B. paintings because she had Alzheimer's disease.

2. Who was Agnes Cott?

Agnes Cott was a witch.

3. What are the teenagers doing at the cemetery at night?

They heart loud music.

4. Why do the villagers think that the old caretaker's house is haunted?

5. Why is the gallery called the Oswald Gallery?

Because of the man who built it in ...

Übung 3: Choose the correct alternative.
Unterstreichen Sie die richtige Variante!

1. The burglar / ~~beggar~~ stole the paintings from the gallery.
2. I was a witness ~~to~~ / for a crime.
3. Michael ~~catched~~ / caught the thief.
4. Can you ~~say me~~ / tell me where the cemetery is?
5. The house looked like / ~~how~~ something from a scary movie.
6. It's my ~~reason~~ / fault the painting was stolen!
7. Lottie ~~felt~~ / ~~fell~~ down the stairs.

fell

Übung 4: Word search. Finden Sie im Suchrätsel sieben Begriffe aus dem Text!

C	H	O	K	I	N	G	T	U	Z
Y	G	V	U	G	T	R	A	J	E
I	O	B	S	H	H	E	B	O	D
S	R	I	C	A	I	K	B	X	W
E	G	R	A	V	E	Y	A	R	D
M	E	X	R	I	F	L	Z	Q	B
I	O	H	Y	C	I	S	S	A	J
Z	U	P	A	I	N	T	I	N	G
O	S	F	L	T	W	A	F	M	E
P	Q	A	G	H	O	S	T	U	C

Übung 5: Translation. Übersetzen Sie!

1. Hintergrund the background
2. Villa the mansiom
3. brennend burning
4. Fingerabdruck fingerprint
5. Leuchten glow
6. seufzen sigh
7. Teufel devil

Übung 6: Unscramble. Bilden Sie sinnvolle Begriffe aus dem Buchstabensalat!

1. The pub in Pendle Lee is called the White chiwt witch.
2. Sergeant Rose has only resadert ~~sarted~~ arrested five people in seven years.
3. Michael looks through the vacrehi archive at the Oswald Gallery.
4. The sagrev graves looked quite scary in the dark.
5. There is a beautiful relacfipe fireplace at Huxley's mansion.
6. The robber almost killed an lederyl elderly woman.

Lösungen

Übung 1: **1.** Felder **2.** Dorf **3.** mitfühlend **4.** alt **5.** Häuschen **6.** geschehen **7.** Tor **8.** Gemälde

Übung 2: **1.** e **2.** g **3.** f **4.** c **5.** b **6.** d **7.** a

Übung 3: **1.** arrived **2.** left **3.** put **4.** heard **5.** thought

Übung 4: **1.** b **2.** c **3.** b

Übung 5: **1.** Where **2.** What **3.** When **4.** Which **5.** Why **6.** Who

Übung 6: **1.** cook **2.** torchlight **3.** pretty **4.** murderer **5.** sell **6.** box **7.** museum **8.** soldier **9.** clue

Übung 7: **1.** e **2.** c **3.** f **4.** h **5.** a **6.** g **7.** i **8.** d **9.** b

Übung 8: **1.** falsch (He's 85.) **2.** richtig **3.** richtig **4.** falsch (No, not without a search warrant.) **5.** falsch (They lost contact much later.) **6.** richtig

Übung 9: **1.** mansion **2.** torch **3.** memory **4.** wallet **5.** cemetery **6.** confident
Lösung: stolen

Übung 10: **1.** thinking **2.** took **3.** wondering **4.** know **5.** off **6.** above

Übung 11: **1.** She **2.** They **3.** We **4.** He **5.** them **6.** us **7.** her **8.** him **9.** you **10.** you

Übung 12: **1.** Sometimes Sylvia couldn't remember their names.
2. Her eyes are the one thing that hasn't changed.
3. Michael climbed through the broken window into the burning house.
4. Neither of the boys had been cut anywhere on their bodies.
5. Perhaps the thief was still in the gallery.

Übung 13: **1.** thieves **2.** women **3.** galleries **4.** information **5.** memories **6.** noises **7.** systems **8.** witches

Abschlusstest

Übung 1: **1.** opened **2.** rush **3.** were hiding **4.** will come **5.** was wearing

Übung 2: **1.** Sylvia Butterworth stole the paintings because she thinks they belong to her.
2. Agnes Cott was burned as a witch at Lancaster Castle in the 17th century.
3. They are bored and are partying at the cemetery. They are lighting candles and listening to music.
4. They think the house is haunted because sometimes strange noises can be heard and light scan be seen at the house.
5. It is named after John Oswald, who built the house the gallery is in.

Übung 3: **1.** burglar **2.** to **3.** caught **4.** tell me **5.** like **6.** fault **7.** fell

Übung 4:

C	H	O	K	I	N	G	T	U	Z
Y	G	V	U	G	T	R	A	J	E
I	O	B	S	H	H	E	B	O	D
S	R	I	C	A	I	K	B	X	W
E	G	R	A	V	E	Y	A	R	D
M	E	X	R	I	F	L	Z	Q	B
I	O	H	Y	C	I	S	S	A	J
Z	U	P	A	I	N	T	I	N	G
O	S	F	L	T	W	A	F	M	E
P	Q	A	G	H	O	S	T	U	C

Übung 5: **1.** background **2.** mansion **3.** burning **4.** fingerprint **5.** glow **6.** sigh 7. devil

Übung 6: **1.** Witch **2.** arrested **3.** archive **4.** graves **5.** fireplace **6.** elderly ~~7. devil~~

Glossar

to admire	bewundern
to alert sb.	jmd. alarmieren, warnen
allotment	Schrebergarten
among	zwischen
apart from	außer
to appear	auftauchen, erscheinen
archive	Archiv
to arrest	verhaften
art restoration	Gemälderestaurierung
at once	*hier*: gleichzeitig
background	Hintergrund
badly	*hier*: sehr, unbedingt
to be about to do sth.	im Begriff sein, etw. zu tun
to be on fire	brennen, in Flammen stehen
to believe	glauben
brave	mutig
to break the law	das Gesetz brechen
bureaucracy	Bürokratie
burglary	Einbruch(diebstahl)
to burgle sth.	einbrechen in
burning	brennend
care	Pflege, Betreuung
caretaker	Hausmeister(in)
cemetery	Friedhof
to chat	plaudern

to choke	ersticken, würgen
church hall	Gemeindesaal
clue	Hinweis, Spur
community	Gemeinschaft
competition	Wettbewerb
confident	selbstsicher
confused	verwirrt
constable	Wachtmeister(in), Polizist(in)
crime	Verbrechen
crime scene	Tatort
Crimestoppers number	Telefonnummer für sachdienliche Hinweise
dare	Mutprobe
database	Datenbank
to deal (dealt, dealt) with	sich beschäftigen mit, zu tun haben mit
detective work	Ermittlungsarbeit
devil	Teufel
to disappear	verschwinden
to disappoint sb.	jmd. enttäuschen
disease	Krankheit
down	*hier*: offen, lose
edge	Rand, Ecke
elderly	älter
emergency	Notfall
to exclaim	ausrufen
exhibition	Ausstellung
to exist	bestehen, existieren
to explore	erkunden

fault	Fehler
file	Akte
filing cabinet	Aktenschrank
fingerprint	Fingerabdruck
fireplace	(offener) Kamin
to flow	fließen
fright	Schreck
to frighten sb.	jmd. erschrecken
ghost	Gespenst
glow	Leuchten
to glow	leuchten
gorgeous	herrlich, wunderschön
grave	Grab
graveyard	Friedhof
to greet sb.	jmd. grüßen
hall	Flur
to hang sb.	jmd. erhängen
to haunt	spuken (in)
headstone	Grabstein
to hide (hid, hidden)	(sich) verstecken
honeymoon	Flitterwochen
housekeeper	Haushälterin
to hurt (hurt, hurt)	verletzen; schmerzen
imagination	Vorstellung
in charge	verantwortlich, zuständig
insulting	beleidigend
to interview	befragen, verhören
investigation	Ermittlung
involved in	beteiligt an
It's none of your business!	Das geht dich nichts an!

Lancashire	engl. Grafschaft, benannt nach der Stadt Lancaster
landscape	Landschaft
magic spell	Zauberspruch
to manage to do sth.	es schaffen, etw. zu tun
mansion	Villa, Herrenhaus
match	*hier*: Treffer
to match with	*hier*: passen zu
meanwhile	währenddessen
memory	Erinnerung
mobile	Handy
nearby	in der Nähe
obsessed (with)	besessen (von)
to offer	(an)bieten
old-fashioned	altmodisch
old people's home	Seniorenheim
to pay sb. a visit	jmd. einen Besuch abstatten
PC (Police Constable)	Wachtmeister(in)
to point to	zeigen auf
prison	Gefängnis
to purr	schnurren
reason	Grund
reception	Empfang
to recognize	erkennen
relieved	erleichtert
to remember sth.	sich erinnern an
right away	sofort
robbery	Raubüberfall
to rush	eilen, sich beeilen
scapegoat	Sündenbock

sculptor	Bildhauer(in)
search warrant	Durchsuchungsbefehl
security	Sicherheit
security camera	Überwachungskamera
serious	ernst
to set (set, set)	*hier*: untergehen
shift	Schicht(dienst)
shocked	schockiert
to sigh	seufzen
siren	Sirene
to smash	zerschlagen, zerschmettern
soldier	Soldat(in)
spider's web	Spinnennetz
spray paint	Sprühfarbe
to steal (stole, stolen)	stehlen
still-life	Stillleben
to stop by	vorbeischauen
straight	direkt, geradewegs
strange	seltsam
stranger	Fremde(r)
to switch on	anschalten
tabby	getigerte Katze
terror alert	Terroralarm
Thank goodness!	Gott sei Dank!
thief	Dieb(in)
to think long and hard	es sich reiflich überlegen
torch	Taschenlampe
trail	Spur
unconscious	bewusstlos
to unpack	auspacken

upset	erschrocken, aufgebracht
to upset (upset, upset) sb.	jmd. ärgern
wallet	Geldbeutel
wavy	gewellt
witch	Hexe
witness	Zeuge/Zeugin
to wonder	sich fragen
to yell	(laut) schreien

Compact Lernkrimis auch in Spanisch, Französisch, Italienisch und Deutsch erhältlich.

Compact Lernkrimi
Classic

A1

A2

B1

Das Rätsel der Mumie
ISBN 978-3-8174-7304-5

Deadly Mistake
ISBN 978-3-8174-8259-7

Die Jagd nach dem Vampir
ISBN 978-3-8174-7305-2

Game Over in Soho
ISBN 978-3-8174-7878-1

Im Schatten des Towers
ISBN 978-3-8174-7687-9

Schüsse im Nebel
ISBN 978-3-8174-7763-0

Toxic Testament
ISBN 978-3-8174-7879-8

American English

Tod im Grand Canyon
ISBN 978-3-8174-7572-8

Sammelband 3 in 1 (B1/B2)

Inspector Hudson ermittelt
ISBN 978-3-8174-7625-1

London Crime Time
ISBN 978-3-8174-7787-6

B2

Das geheimnisvolle Gemälde
ISBN 978-3-8174-7306-9

Die Spur des Höllenhundes
ISBN 978-3-8174-7307-6

Diebstahl im Morgengrauen
ISBN 978-3-8174-7638-1

Lady Mayfairs Rache
ISBN 978-3-8174-7815-6

Business English

Das letzte Roulette
ISBN 978-3-8174-7609-1

Der 25-Millionen-Dollar-Coup
ISBN 978-3-8174-7659-6

Schmierige Geschäfte
ISBN 978-3-8174-7658-9

Teuflische Intrigen
ISBN 978-3-8174-7608-4

American English

Das Skyline-Syndikat
ISBN 978-3-8174-7573-5

C1 / C2

A Scottish Murder Mystery
ISBN 978-3-8174-8379-2

Compact Lernkrimi
Kurzkrimis

Compact Lernkrimi
Mystery

Compact Lernkrimi
Thriller

			A1
Blood and Breakfast ISBN 978-3-8174-7760-9 **Endstation Waterloo Bridge** ISBN 978-3-8174-7733-3 **Es war Mord, my Lord** ISBN 978-3-8174-7734-0 **Mord at Teatime** ISBN 978-3-8174-7839-2			A2
Death Comes Knocking ISBN 978-3-8174-7945-0	**Der rote Nebel** ISBN 978-3-8174-7574-2	**Ein fast perfekter Coup** ISBN 978-3-8174-7568-1 **Komplott unter Palmen** ISBN 978-3-8174-7571-1	B1
	Der Seelenjäger ISBN 978-3-8174-7581-0	**Die genetische Falle** ISBN 978-3-8174-7569-8 **Schatten der Vergangenheit** ISBN 978-3-8174-7570-4	B2
			C1 / C2

Compact Lernkrimi History

Compact Lernkrimi Hörbuch

	Compact Lernkrimi History	Compact Lernkrimi Hörbuch
A1		
A2		**A Shot in the Night** ISBN 978-3-8174-8202-3 **Death Wish** ISBN 978-3-8174-8204-7 **The Butterworth Mystery** ISBN 978-3-8174-8203-0
B1	**Der Rächer von Canterbury** ISBN 978-3-8174-7662-6 **Tod eines Dandys** ISBN 978-3-8174-7660-2	**Das Mädchen von King's Cross** ISBN 978-3-8174-7673-2 **Der Themse-Mörder** ISBN 978-3-8174-7674-9
B2	**Der unheimliche Ritter** ISBN 978-3-8174-7661-9 **Die Rache des Lords** ISBN 978-3-8174-7663-3	**Blutige Erbschaft** ISBN 978-3-8174-7676-3 **Die Intrigantin** ISBN 978-3-8174-7675-6 **Business English** **Mord im Office** ISBN 978-3-8174-7747-0
C1 / C2		

Compact Lernkrimi
Audio-Learning

Compact Lernkrimi
Sprachkurs

Compact Lernkrimi Audio-Learning	Compact Lernkrimi Sprachkurs	
	Englisch für Anfänger (A1/A2) ISBN 978-3-8174-7784-5	A1
Verschollen im Dartmoor ISBN 978-3-8174-7796-8		A2
Totenstille im Hyde Park ISBN 978-3-8174-7797-5		B1
		B2
		C1 / C2